The Great Pyramid of Giza

Author: Anne Millard

WORLD ALMANAC® LIBRARY

Please visit our web site at: **www.worldalmanaclibrary.com**
For a free color catalog describing World Almanac® Library's list
of high-quality books and multimedia programs, call 1-800-848-2928 (USA)
or 1-800-387-3178 (Canada). World Almanac® Library's fax: (414) 332-3567.

Library of Congress Cataloging-in-Publication Data

Millard, Anne.
  The great pyramid of Giza / by Anne Millard.
    p. cm. — (Places in history)
  Includes index.
  ISBN 0-8368-5811-5 (lib. bdg.)
  ISBN 0-8368-5818-2 (softcover)
  1. Great Pyramid (Egypt)—Juvenile literature. 2. Pyramids of Giza (Egypt)—Juvenile literature. 3. Egypt—
Antiquities—Juvenile literature. 4. Egypt—Civilization—To 332 B.C.—Juvenile literature. I. Title. II. Series.
  DT63.M5155 2005
  932—dc22   2004056926

First published in 2005 by
World Almanac® Library
330 West Olive Street, Suite 100
Milwaukee, WI 53212 USA

Consultant: Helen Strudwick

Photo credits: Alamy: 32, 33L, 35R; Art Archive: 1, 5L, 6, 9, 11T, 11B, 13L, 14, 15L, 16, 17L, 17R, 18L, 19L, 19R, 20R,
21BR, 22B, 23B, 26, 27L, 27R, 28T, 28–9, 30, 37L, 38, 40, 43T; British Museum: 25BL; Corbis: 2–3, 21T, 21BL, 25BR,
33R, 34T, 34B, 42, 44, 45T; Heritage Images: 23T, 39R; National Geographic: 15R, 18–19, 24T, 24B, 31T, 36, 39T;
Werner Forman 5R, 12, 13R, 22TR.

Printed in the United States of America

1 2 3 4 5 6 7 8 9 09 08 07 06 05

Contents

Introduction

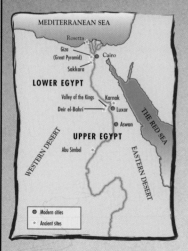

The Great Pyramid certainly lives up to its name. It is huge! It was originally 482 feet (147 meters) tall, and its sides measured just over 755 feet (230 meters) at its base. It is estimated that more than two million blocks of stone were used to build it. Even today—when people are used to large buildings—they still gaze in wonder at the Great Pyramid's majestic bulk. It is easy to wonder why the ancient Egyptians spent so much time, energy, and resources on building such a colossal monument.

Why Was It Built?

The Great Pyramid is the tomb of a king of Upper and Lower Egypt—Khufu—who lived in about 2600 B.C. The Great Pyramid had several different purposes and a number of different symbolic meanings, as did most things in ancient Egyptian religious beliefs. The ancient Egyptians believed that when they died, they were reborn into the Next World—which was said to be like the Egypt they loved but made perfect. To enjoy life properly in the Next World, the Egyptians believed that a person's spirit needed to return to its body occasionally. That was why they invented the process of mummification—a way to preserve the body after death.

An Elaborate Tomb

The Egyptians also believed that they could take all the things they needed to live comfortably in the Next World by placing these objects in their tombs. The Great Pyramid was the king's tomb, specially designed to give maximum protection to his body and his treasure. It also provided a place where priests could make offerings to his spirit. The pyramid and any treasure in it also had a symbolic significance, displaying the power and glory of the king to his people, future generations, and the gods. The Egyptians believed that their king was more than just a man. They considered him to be an earthly form of the god Horus (who had once ruled Egypt himself). This made the king a sacred, part-divine being who would become a god himself after death. From heaven, according to Egyptian beliefs, the king was thought to go on

The pyramids and the Sphinx are silhouetted against the changing colors of the evening sky as Ra sinks in glory into the West and enters the Underworld. He will be reborn in the East in the morning.

caring for his subjects, just as he had done on Earth. The pyramid was also regarded as the Earthly gateway through which the king's spirit would pass before joining the gods in the Next World.

A Gateway to the Next World

Egypt's priests taught that, in the beginning, there was nothing but water. Then, the god Atum, who lived in this ocean, thrust up the first land. The sungod, Ra, stood on this mound of land and created the whole world and everything in it. The mound was Ra's most holy symbol, and the Egyptians saw it as a symbol not only of creation and birth but also of rebirth into the Next World. What better place to bury a king than under a pyramid—a representation of the

The interior walls of this pyramid, which belongs to one of Khufu's descendents, are covered with the spells, prayers, and hymns from the Pyramid Texts.

sun god's holy symbol? The word "pyramid" comes from an ancient Greek word. The Egyptian equivalent was originally "mr," meaning "a place of ascension." An Egyptian text, known as the *Pyramid Texts*, states: "I have trodden on the sun's rays, using them as a ramp to go up . . . ." So, even though a pyramid does not reach all the way to heaven, it symbolizes a ramp made of sunbeams that would carry a king to join the god Ra.

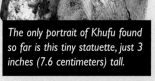

The only portrait of Khufu found so far is this tiny statuette, just 3 inches (7.6 centimeters) tall.

CHAPTER 1

How It Was Built

No evidence exists that verifies the exact building methods used by the ancient Egyptians, but many highly plausible theories have been considered over the years. We know that, whatever the method, a pyramid would have taken a long time to build. Therefore, when Khufu came to the throne, one of his very first acts would have been to order the building of his pyramid. The Egyptians did not have cranes or mechanical excavators, but they did have great ingenuity.

This 19th-century illustration shows a village at the foot of the Giza Plateau. The waters of the Nile River's annual Inundation crept up to the foot of the Plateau until the building of modern dams at Aswan.

One of the first people to write about visiting Egypt was a Greek named Herodotus, who visited Egypt in about 450 B.C. His book reports that Khufu was a cruel tyrant who oppressed his people and reduced the country to poverty in order to build his pyramid. An earlier papyrus from about 1900 B.C. gives a similar impression of Khufu. It is also possible, however, that Herodotus had a deep distrust of eastern kings because of the suffering inflicted on the Greeks by the Persians.

Location

The choice of site for Khufu's pyramid was important. Sakkara, the nearest site to the capital, already had Zoser's Step Pyramid, and Khufu's father, Sneferu, had built his pyramid to the south, at Dahshur. Khufu preferred the Giza Plateau for his pyramid.

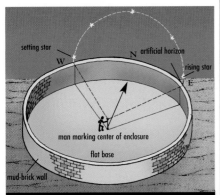

The Egyptians believed a pyramid's sides needed to precisely face north, south, east, and west, so calculations had to be made very carefully.

This site had several advantages. The rocky plateau rose sharply above the river valley, making it very imposing. It was nearly flat, made of good, solid stone to build on, and located near plenty of local limestone, from which the pyramid could be built. It was also only a few miles north of Memphis, the capital.

Planning

The first job would probably have been to draw up a plan for the king's approval. Presumably, the next challenge would have been to determine which direction was north. Many historians think this would have been necessary because ancient Egyptians believed the pyramid had to have each side perfectly oriented with one of the points of the compass for the rituals to work properly. To find north, surveyors would probably have first built a round, high-walled enclosure out of mud-brick (see diagram, left). A priest-surveyor then probably stood at the center of the circle. When a particular star first appeared in the sky (rising star), just above the eastern wall (artificial horizon), his assistant would have marked the spot in the ground. The pair would then have had to wait to mark the point where the star set in the west (setting star). These two points and the place where the priest had stood then formed a triangle—the angle of which would have been divided to give them the measurement for north. The pyramid's sides would have

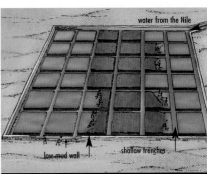

Next, the site would be divided into squares. Water-filled channels would be used as a guide for clearing a smooth surface.

then been marked out on the ground. The area would then have been divided into sections with channels cut between them and filled with water (see diagram, above). Then, workmen would have cut away all the rock until it was level with the surface

The Great Pyramid of Giza

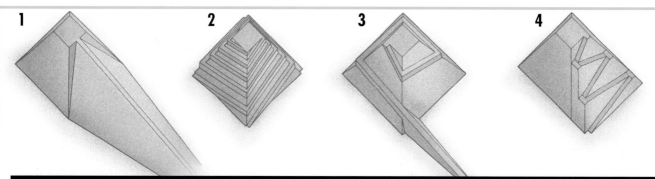

There are several theories about how ramps were constructed. Four are illustrated here: (1) a straight, sloping ramp up one face; (2) several ramps starting at the base and wrapping around the pyramid; (3) a single ramp wrapping around the pyramid; (4) a zigzag-ramp on one side of the pyramid.

of the water. After the water would have been drained out and the small channels filled in, they would have a flat surface, exactly oriented for pyramid-building to start.

Mountains of Stone

The moment Khufu decided to build his pyramid at Giza, the order would have gone out to start cutting stones.

The limestone for the body of the pyramid would have been quarried at Giza itself, but the fine, white limestone for the casing blocks came from Turah, a quarry on the other side of the Nile. The great slabs of granite for the burial chamber came from Aswan, which is about 600 miles (965 kilometers) to the south. Other stones, such as gleaming alabaster and black basalt, came from quarries in Egypt's deserts. By the

time the site was leveled and the main workforce arrived, hundreds of blocks would have been ready and waiting.

Heavy Work

The average weight of the 2.3 million stone blocks in the Great Pyramid is 2.5 tons (2.3 tonnes), but some weigh 15 tons (13.6 tonnes) or more. To get a block of stone into place, it would have been levered onto a sled and secured with ropes. A gang of 10

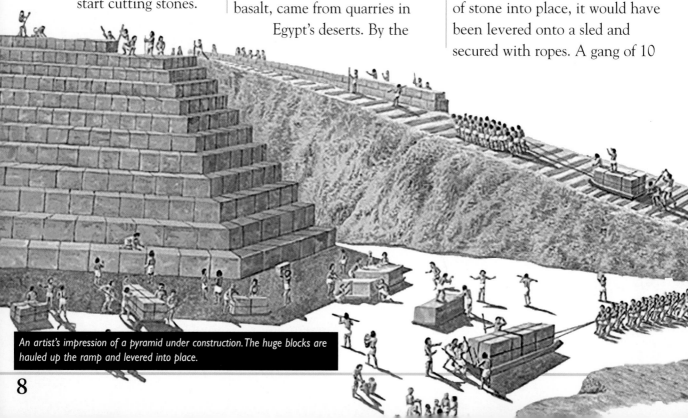

An artist's impression of a pyramid under construction. The huge blocks are hauled up the ramp and levered into place.

Tales & Customs — Getting the Facts Straight

The myth that Hebrew slaves built the Great Pyramid during their period in Egypt was started by the Jewish writer Flavius Josephus (c. A.D. 37–100), who wrote several books to explain Jewish religion and history to non-Jewish readers. In fact, the pyramids were built more than one thousand years before the period the Jews of the Near East settled in Egypt. Although much is shrouded in mystery, there is a wealth of archaeological evidence that supports what is commonly accepted to be the time of the Great Pyramid's origins.

or more men, depending on the size of the block, would then grasp the ropes and haul it along. Another gang of men would walk in front of the stone-hauling team, laying rollers so the sled would glide along more easily. The workers poured down milk, which is greasy, to help the sled glide over the rollers. Water may have been splashed onto the rollers because the friction of the sled on the rollers could cause the rollers to smolder.

Painstaking Construction

The first blocks were laid in the center of the pyramid's base, and then the rest of the first layer of stones was placed around them. Finally, the casing stones were positioned on the outside. A ramp of mud bricks, sand, and rubble would then have been built so that the

next layer of stones could be pulled into place. The ramp would be extended, layer upon layer, until the required height was reached. Finally, a pyramid-shaped capstone would have been placed on top. Some scholars suggest that the capstone would have been covered with gold, which would dazzle people in the hot Egyptian sun. The ramps were then removed from top to bottom, and the casing stones cut to the correct angle. Experts disagree as to how many ramps were used and how they were placed. Some think just one very long ramp was used. Others believe ramps were built around the four sides of the pyramid as it rose. Whatever method was used, it was a huge job shifting all those blocks. According to one estimate,

workmen would have needed to get one block in place every two minutes. Even when the main pyramid was finished, work was still far from over. A pyramid was simply one part of a whole complex of connected buildings—all of which were vitally important for running the funeral cult after the burial of the king.

Although the casing blocks have been taken from most of the pyramids, the patches that remain show how tightly they fitted with one another.

The ideas and expertise required for building the Great Pyramid can be traced back to the beginning of Egyptian civilization. The ancient Egyptians did not need help from visitors from other planets or survivors of an older, "lost" civilization, as some people have suggested. We can trace their efforts at making tombs from simple beginnings, through successes and failures, right up to the Great Pyramid.

Egypt's First Graves

The first "ancient Egyptian" graves—dated to c. 5000 B.C.— were just oval scoops in the sand. A body was wrapped in linen or a mat and surrounded with provisions for the Next World. A mound of sand and stones was raised over the top. The poor went on being buried like that throughout Egyptian history, but as Egypt grew rich, its leaders— chiefs and then kings—wanted bigger, more impressive monuments.

Early Mastabas

These graves were cut deeper and in a neater rectangular shape. The sides were lined with wood or mud bricks and the body was placed in a reed or wooden coffin. The mound over the top was also better made, and it was eventually replaced by a rectangular mud-brick building, the sides of which sloped in slightly. This style of tomb was called a "mastaba." The royal mastabas had stone-lined burial chambers surrounded by many rooms,

A very ancient Egyptian. He was buried with supplies of food and drink and his prized possessions in a shallow grave. The hot desert sand dried out his body and preserved it for about 5,000 years.

Time Line

c. 5000–3100 B.C.

The Predynastic Period. Egypt is a land of small states that come together into two kingdoms—Upper and Lower Egypt. At first, people are buried in scoops in the sand, but Egyptian graves evolve into mud-brick mastabas.

c. 3100–2686 B.C.

The Archaic Period. Narmer, King of Upper Egypt, conquers the North, and Egypt is united. Dynasties I and II. Kings are buried in large mud-brick mastabas. Memphis is the capital.

The pyramid at Meidum had a stepped core, but with straight sides on the outside. The outer casing collapsed, and the inner stepped structure is now visible.

all full with food, tools, weapons, furniture, clothes, and jewelry.

The First Pyramids

About 2670 B.C., an architect named Imhotep built a square, stone mastaba for his king, Zoser. Imhotep enlarged the mastaba and added other, smaller mastabas on top, thus forming the first "step" pyramid. Within seventy years there was another attempt to improve the design of the

kings' funeral monuments. The steps of the last step pyramid (thought to belong to Huni, the last King of Dynasty II) were filled in with sloping blocks. This design was a disaster—the outer casing fell away, dragging much of the inside of the pyramid with it.

The early kings thought their spirits would join the Pole Star and the stars that cluster around it above the North Pole. They called them "the imperishable

stars," because they never sank below the horizon, making them good symbols of eternity.

But as the Sun god Ra grew in importance, tomb design had to change again to aid passage to Ra's side in the afterlife. New tombs were planned as perfectly shaped pyramids. But this design

c. 2682–2181 B.C.

The Old Kingdom. Dynasties III to VI. A time of great achievement. The Step Pyramid is built. From Dynasty IV onwards, pyramids have straight sides. This is when the Giza pyramids were built.

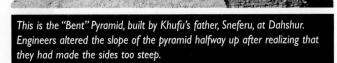

This is the "Bent" Pyramid, built by Khufu's father, Sneferu, at Dahshur. Engineers altered the slope of the pyramid halfway up after realizing that they had made the sides too steep.

The Great Pyramid of Giza

Time and weather have not been kind to the Sphinx. Windblown sand constantly erodes its body and vandals have knocked off its nose.

also resulted in disaster! The angle of the sides was too steep. In order to finish it, the architects had to change to a gentler slope, which left them with a bent structure. Undaunted, they made another attempt and, this time, triumphed. This pyramid became the final resting place of Sneferu, Khufu's father.

The Pharaohs

When Khufu died, his son Radjedef came to the throne. The new king immediately started to build his own pyramid at Abu Roash, north of Giza. Radjedef had only a brief reign, and his pyramid was never finished. He was succeeded by his younger brother, Khafre, who built the second major pyramid at Giza. This pyramid was not quite as tall as the Great Pyramid—as his father Khufu's pyramid has come to be known. But because it is on slightly higher

c. 2181–2025 B.C.

The First Intermediate Period. Dynasties VII to X. Egypt descends into chaos with rival kings, civil wars, powerful warlords, and famines.

c. 2025–1700 B.C.

The Middle Kingdom. Dynasties XI to XIII. Egypt is reunited by a prince of Thebes. Thebes becomes the capital and royal tombs are under great temples. Dynasty XII kings move back north to a site near Memphis and are buried in pyramids. Another period of great cultural achievement.

ground, it looks taller, especially because some of its casing blocks remain at the top, whereas all Khufu's have since been removed.

A great deal of stone had been quarried at Giza, leaving a large rocky outcrop close to where Khafre's Valley Temple was being built. Someone whose identity is not known suggested carving this stone into a statue of a sphinx—a lion with a human head. The face of the Sphinx may be a portrait of King Khafre.

The Sphinx was a form of the Sun god who was thought to guard the site. A temple dedicated to him was built in front of its paws. Khafre's son, Menkawre, also built a pyramid at Giza, but his was yet smaller than his father's. The three Giza pyramids follow the line of the solid rock of the plateau, so each one is set slightly back from the other, and each has its own clear view of the North, to establish the exact position the priests required.

Beautifully carved hieroglyphics in the chambers of later pyramids give us vital clues about religious beliefs in the time of Khufu and in the hundreds of years before him.

Khufu's Heirs

Only one other major royal monument was erected at Giza—that of Queen Khentkawes. A rocky outcrop was carved into a square platform and then a mastaba-like tomb was built on top. Queen Khentkawes may have reigned on her own for a while. Her two sons were the first kings of Dynasty V.

The kings of Dynasties V and VI also built pyramids, but none of them are anywhere near as big as those at Giza nor were they as well-built. Their inner blocks are small, and over the years some have collapsed.

However, a dramatic discovery was made in the chamber of the pyramid of Unas, the last king of Dynasty V. The walls were covered in inscriptions. These inscriptions are now known as the *Pyramid Texts*, and they include spells, prayers, and rituals. Some date back to the time when rulers were buried in the desert sand. Another, obviously dating from the time of the great mud-brick mastabas, assures the

c. 1700–1550 B.C.
The Second Intermediate Period. Dynasties XIV to XVII.
The Hyksos invade and conquer much of Egypt.
Only Thebes retains some independence.

This figurine from the troubled First Intermediate period shows an emaciated figure in the midst of famine.

The Great Pyramid of Giza

king, "The bricks are removed for you from the great tomb." These texts give us vital clues about earlier beliefs.

Decline and Fall

The great age of pyramid building—Dynasties II through VI—is known as the Old Kingdom. At the end of the Old Kingdom, Egypt suffered a troubled time called the First Intermediate Period, during which there were civil wars, famine, and general lawlessness. Offerings in all the Mortuary Temples stopped. The authority of the kings broke down and tomb robbers were out in abundance. Even the Giza pyramids were broken into.

During the First Intermediate Period, few kings lived long enough to build tombs, but some managed a small pyramid. Meanwhile the Giza giants remained, reminding people of what had been achieved in the days when Egypt was a prosperous, united country.

New Pyramids and Ancient Tourists

Most Middle Kingdom pyramids were made of mud bricks with a casing of stone. Once the casing was gone, the wind and sand slowly destroyed the bricks, leaving odd shapes. The Middle Kingdom, like the Old Kingdom, collapsed. Egypt's Second Intermediate Period was even worse than the First Intermediate Period. The northern part of Egypt was taken over for more than one hundred years by people from the East known as the Hyksos.

The prosperous New Kingdom period began when the princes of Thebes drove the Hyksos out. As a consequence, Thebes was made the new capital of Egypt. Just before the beginning of the New Kingdom, kings were buried on the West Bank of the Nile, at Luxor, in tombs described by the Egyptians as pyramids, but this soon changed to tombs cut into the floor and cliff faces of a remote valley that we know as the Valley of the Kings. Interestingly, the mountain that towers over this valley is shaped exactly like a pyramid. Thebes is too far south to be a convenient site for the capital of a long, narrow country like Egypt. In the New Kingdom, Thebes remained the greatest of their holy cities, the center of the worship of Amun, King of the Gods, and the burial place of kings, queens, other members of the royal family, and nobles. Royalty visited

In the Pyramid Age, coffins and sarcophagi were rectangular in shape. By the New Kingdom, a new style prevailed, and people were buried in anthropoid coffins.

The Sphinx towers above the temple built in its honor. It contains the stela that tells the story of the Sphinx and Prince Tuthmosis.

appeared to him in a dream and said that if the prince would have the sand—which had buried the Sphinx up to its neck—cleared away, he would make the prince King of Egypt. The prince did as requested. All his elder brothers died, and he became King Tuthmosis IV. He set up a big stela in a little chapel between the paws of the Sphinx, recounting the story of his dream. Besides the problem with the sand, the body of the Sphinx was crumbling in places, and work was done to repair it. This was the first in a series of repairs that took place in the Late Period, under the Greeks and Romans, and again in the 20th century. Eventually, the New Kingdom declined, Egypt lost its empire and entered the

the site for festivals and funerals, but the government was run from Memphis, which meant that the court was once more in the shadow (almost literally) of the Giza pyramids. By this time, the Giza pyramids and other Old Kingdom pyramids were more than 1,000 years old and a popular tourist destination. One tourist was a scribe who wrote on a wall that he had visited a pyramid and found it so beautiful, "as though heaven were within it and the Sun rising in it."

The Sphinx's Promise

According to legend, one day a prince fell asleep in the shadow of the great Sphinx at Giza. The Sphinx

664–332 B.C.
The Late Period. Dynasty XXVI to XXX. A native Egyptian dynasty rules and breaks away from the Assyrian Empire, renewing Egypt's greatness. Its capital is Sais. Egypt is twice invaded and becomes part of the Persian Empire, though native rulers constantly try, sometimes successfully, to assert their independence.

The Great Pyramid was a constant reminder to later generations of Khufu's glory. Perhaps it inspired later kings to build huge monuments of their own.

The Great Pyramid of Giza

These steep-sided pyramids at Meroe in modern-day Sudan are, like so many others, directly influenced by the pyramids at Giza.

Third Intermediate Period, during which a small temple was built against the pyramid of one of Khufu's Queens. It was dedicated to the goddess Isis. Meanwhile, the pyramid tradition had found its way south, to the Egyptian province of Nubia. Nubia gained its independence and had its own kings. They and their successors, the kings of the great Kingdom of Meroe, were buried in steep sided stone pyramids at Nuri, el Kurru, and Meroe itself, which is in the modern Sudan.

Egyptian greatness was reestablished in the Late Period. The Egyptians began studying their ancient history and copying Old Kingdom art styles. They also revived old cults, including those of Khufu, Khafre, and Menkawre.

Wonder of the World

Late Period kings started hiring Greek soldiers to fight for them, and Greek merchants soon flocked to Egypt. Later, Greek

Time line

332–330 B.C.
The Ptolemic Period. Egypt is conquered by Alexander the Great. After Alexander's death, his general, Ptolemy, becomes Egypt's king. Alexandria is built and is the capital. The last ruler descended from Ptolemy, the great Cleopatra VII, is defeated by the Romans.

30 B.C.–A.D. 641
Egypt is part of the Roman and Byzantine (beginning in A.D. 395) Empires, during which Egypt becomes Christian.

A.D. 641–present The Islamic Period.

and Roman tourists came, fascinated by the history and "strangeness" of the ancient Egyptian culture. Some well-traveled Greeks compiled a list of the most spectacular things they had seen in countries around the Mediterranean—the Seven Wonders of the World. The Giza pyramids are on the list. They were by far the oldest pyramids, but they are the only ones to have survived more or less intact to the present day. In 332 B.C., Alexander the Great conquered Egypt. The family of his general, Ptolemy, then ruled Egypt for about 300 years, until they were overthrown by the Romans. Egypt stayed under the rule of the Romans and their successors in the Middle East, the Byzantines, until the arrival of Muslim invaders in A.D. 641.

Blocks from the pyramids were used to build Cairo's defenses. This shows part of the magnificent walls that guard the Citadel in Cairo. It is built on an outcrop of rock overlooking the city.

A Stone Quarry

The new rulers were fascinated by the Giza pyramids, especially by the thought that they contained treasure. In the 9th century, the Muslim ruler Ma'mun ordered his men to break into the pyramids. However, any treasure that had once been there had been stolen or removed thousands of years previously. In 969, a new line of Muslim rulers called the Fatimids came to power. They decided to build and fortify a new capital for themselves at Cairo. Nearby were the Giza pyramids, with all their finely cut casing blocks. Having this building material so close by proved too tempting to the Fatimids. The casing blocks of the Great Pyramid can be seen today in the walls of Cairo.

Alexander the Great, King of Macedon. When he conquered Egypt, Alexander visited the oasis of Siwa in order to consult the oracle of the god Amun. It is believed the oracle confirmed that Alexander was actually Amun's son.

CHAPTER 3

Exploring the Pyramids

Gazing up at the huge kings' pyramids at Giza is awe inspiring, and there is even more to see inside them. Each pyramid had around it a complex of temples, facilities for the people involved in building the pyramid, and other structures. The Great Pyramid itself is well-preserved, but much of its complex has been lost. Fortunately, examples of temples and other important buildings from later pyramid complexes still exist.

Pages 20–21: Inside the Great Pyramid

Boat museum

5

4

3

2

1

9

Sphinx

6

13

11

12

The Great Pyramid of Giza

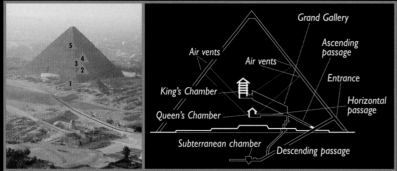

This 19th-century engraving shows the entrance to the Horizontal Passage, with the Grand Gallery above it.

 Subterranean Chamber

The internal design of the Great Pyramid differs from all other pyramids. It was once thought that it had three chambers because the plans changed during construction, but it is now thought that they were all intended from the start. The lowest room, the Subterranean Chamber, was cut into the solid rock of the plateau and is reached by the Descending Passage. Researchers are not sure what this chamber was for, but some think it may have been related to the king's passage to the Next World and his well-being there.

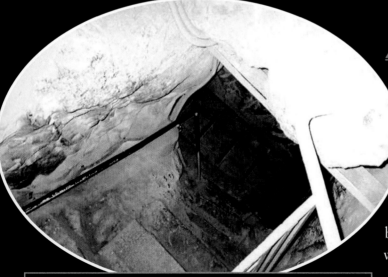

The passages in the Great Pyramid—such as the Ascending Passage, which leads to both the Horizontal Passage and the Grand Gallery—are often very narrow.

2 Queen's Chamber

The Ascending Passage is very small, so people have to bend down to get through it. It leads to the Horizontal Passage, which connects to the Queen's Chamber. Despite its name, this room was never intended for the burial of a queen. It was probably where a statue of the king was placed.

"Air Vents"

Leading out of the King's and Queen's Chambers are two passages, just eight inches (20 cm) on each side, one in the north wall and one in the south wall. Although they have been dubbed "air vents," neither of these passages reaches the outside of the pyramid, and they have nothing to do with bringing air into the pyramid. They are thought to be symbolic passages by which the royal spirit could travel to the stars. A tiny robot has explored the air vents in the Queen's Chamber and found doors at the end—the gates to heaven.

A robot designed specifically for investigating the curious "air vents" in the Great Pyramid is sent into the "vent" leading out of the Queen's Chamber.

Grand Gallery

Also opening off the Ascending Passage is the magnificent Grand Gallery. At the top is the Antechamber, where three slabs of granite are stored. After the burial these were slid into place, sealing off the burial chamber beyond.

The King's Chamber still contains the bottom half of Khufu's sarcophagus.

King's Chamber

The King's Chamber measures approximately 33 by 16 by 16 feet (10 by 5 by 5 meters) and is built from granite blocks from Aswan. Nine granite slabs span the roof, each 16 feet (5 m) long and weighing between 55,125 and 88,200 pounds (25,000 and 40,000 kilograms). The King's sarcophagus is made of red granite and was placed at the west end of the room.

Passing through the Grand Gallery involves a very steep climb up to the King's Chamber.

The Great Pyramid of Giza

Although Khufu's Valley Temple has been destroyed, the massive rose-granite pillars of Khafre's temple still stand.

 Valley Temple

The architects placed the Valley Temple at the point where the desert met the fertile farming land watered by the Nile. It is thought that the king's body may have been mummified in this temple. Khufu's Valley Temple has long since disappeared, but that of his son, Khafre, who built the second pyramid at Giza, has survived. The ground floor of Khafre's Valley Temple contains chambers and a spectacular columned hall. The floor is made of alabaster and the columns are huge blocks of granite. In the late 1980s, the Egyptian government funded a new sewage system for the modern town that stands at the foot of the Giza Plateau. When the laborers started digging trenches they found a pavement of black basalt stone, which is all that is left of Khufu's Valley Temple.

 Causeway

Leading up to the Valley Temple of any pyramid is the Causeway—a long covered processional road, decorated with beautifully carved reliefs. Khufu's Causeway has been demolished over the centuries, but traces of it were found at the same time as the pavement of his Valley Temple was discovered. Only a few shattered pieces of Khufu's reliefs, which were reused by a later king in another pyramid, have been found.

Although the Great Pyramid's Causeway has been destroyed, we can gain a sense of its grandeur from Pharaoh Unas's Causeway at Sakkara.

▲8 Mortuary Temple

The Mortuary Temple was built close to the east side of the pyramid. Some of the funeral rites were probably celebrated there. After the king's funeral, offerings would have been made there by the priests every day thereafter—or that was the intention. It has been suggested that, at least in later pyramids, the Mortuary Temple may also be seen as a symbolic palace for the king to use in the afterlife. Khufu's Mortuary Temple has been destroyed, but enough of it remains to show that it was an impressive building.

Beside the Sphinx is Khafre's Valley Temple. It has two doors. This is the one used by tourists.

This well-preserved chair from Hetep-heres' tomb is one of many beautiful items excavated at Giza.

▲9 QUEENS' PYRAMIDS

Recent excavations have revealed that outside the southeast corner of Khufu's pyramid was a smaller one, only 66 feet (20 m) long on each side. This pyramid is believed to have been for the King's "ka," or part of his soul. To the east of this pyramid are three larger pyramids that were built for Khufu's queens. Each has a passage leading down to an antechamber and a burial chamber. Close by, at the bottom of a deep shaft, were found the remains of the body of Khufu's mother, Hetep-heres.

 ## Barracks for Unskilled Laborers

The unskilled laborers who worked on the pyramids lived in barracks on the western edge of the site at Giza. These barracks contained kitchens, stores, and social areas, as well as workshops for the craftsmen. In order to get the stone that came from distant quarries and all the other supplies that were needed as close to the building site as possible, a huge harbor was excavated at the foot of the plateau. Hundreds of men were needed to dig out the massive harbor, which was then lined with stone, but it reduced the distance that stone and supplies had to be dragged overland. Water was supplied to the harbor by a canal connected to the Nile. This canal, in itself, was an amazing feat of engineering.

The massive wall now called the Wall of the Crow divided the workmen's village from the sacred site at Giza.

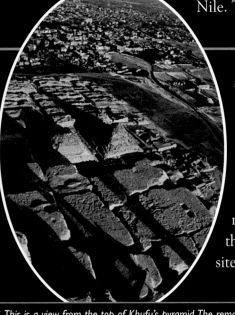

Ancient Site of Khufu's Palace

Khufu needed a palace in which he could stay when he came to visit the site and inspect the progress of the work. It may not have been as large as the one at Memphis, but it still had to be fit for the god-king, his family, chief courtiers, and servants. It was built to the east of the pyramid, with the Valley Temple to the north and the harbor to the south. Giza must have been one of the noisiest, dustiest sites in Egypt. Some of the noise and dust must have penetrated into the cool comfort of the palace.

This is a view from the top of Khufu's pyramid. The remains of what may have been Khufu's palace are visible nearby.

12   Old Khufu Settlement

The craftsmen had to have proper houses for themselves and their families. Even after the king's burial, craftsmen were still needed to provide new ritual vessels for the priests and to make repairs. The priests, their families, and their descendents, who would make offerings to Khufu's spirit, expected to be given large, comfortable houses near their places of work. The architects, therefore, designed "Gerget Khufu," the Settlement of Khufu, pleasantly situated on the south side of the harbor with rolling fields beyond its eastern boundary. Like the remains of Khufu's Valley Temple, the remains of the town, the palace, and the harbor were located during the great sewer installation project of the 1980s and 1990s.

In the late 20th century, the remains of Giza's old settlement were excavated. This is where the pyramids' many craftsmen and their families were housed.

Statues like this one of Hetep-heres and her husband Katep were placed in the statue chambers of tombs.

13   Nobles' Mastabas

Impressive tombs also had to be built for the other members of the royal family and the most important courtiers. These tombs were large stone mastabas. The rooms were decorated with top-quality relief carvings that were painted in bright colors. The mastabas were arranged in neat rows, like houses along streets. The more important you were, the closer your mastaba was to the king's pyramid. This was so Khufu would have the services of his family and courtiers in the Next World, as in this one.

Noblemen and other people of importance were buried in elaborate tombs called mastabas.

We know very little about the personalities and private lives of the royal family of Dynasty IV, because so few written documents survived from their time. The Egyptians believed that if you wrote something down, it would go on happening. So, they were careful not to record things like rebellions or family feuds among the royal family. We do, however, know a little about some members of the royal family, the Egyptian gods, and the people who helped build the pyramids from the artifacts they left behind.

This gilded chest filled with silver bracelets decorated with jewel-encrusted butterflies was discovered in Queen Hetep-heres' tomb at Giza.

The Royal Family

Khufu is thought to have had three queens, hence the three pyramids beside his at Giza. The chief queen was his sister-wife Meritites, who was the mother of Crown Prince Kawab and Hetep-heres II. Kawab died before his father, and Redjedef, son of Khufu by another queen, became king. He reigned only a short time and was succeeded by Khafre, the son of the third queen of Khufu. Khafre had at least two queens. One was his niece, Meresankh III, daughter of Kawab and Hetep-heres II. The other queen bore Khafre's heir, Menkawre.

Based on evidence gleaned from their mastaba tombs, some scholars believe there was a power struggle for the throne between Redjedef and Khafre and that the feud persisted between their children. If there was such a feud, it was healed when Userkaf, who was thought to be descended from Redjedef and was the first king of Dynasty V, married Khentkawes, daughter of Menkawre.

Earthly Gods

Kings were considered so holy, so full of magic power, that even to touch one by mistake was believed to be able to kill a person. It was believed that the gods gave the king the authority, the power, and the wisdom to rule well. Kings were even believed to be able to control the Inundation and ensure a good annual flood to water the fields. To enforce his policies and carry out the day-to-day business of

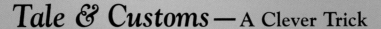

According to legend, when men plotted against Ra, the Sun god, he sent the goddess Hathor to punish them. She transformed herself into Sekhmet, a fierce lioness, and set about killing all the humans. Alarmed by this, Ra had 7,000 jars of beer dyed red to look like blood and flooded the fields with it. Sekhmet, thinking it was blood, lapped it up, became very drunk and happy and turned back into the lovely, gentle Hathor. Humanity was saved.

government, the king used hundreds of officials. All the top posts in government in Dynasty IV were held by the kings' relatives—uncles, brothers, and cousins. These officials had their own staffs to advise them and to do the actual work.

The Planners

The most important official, the head of all branches of the government, was the vizier. The vizier had total responsibility for the pyramid

A statue of a seated scribe holding a roll of papyrus across his knees. His well-fed appearance gives an impression of success in life.

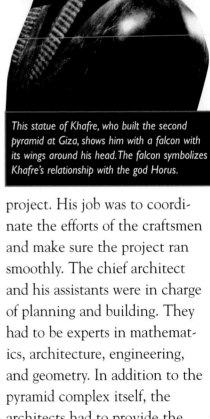

This statue of Khafre, who built the second pyramid at Giza, shows him with a falcon with its wings around his head. The falcon symbolizes Khafre's relationship with the god Horus.

project. His job was to coordinate the efforts of the craftsmen and make sure the project ran smoothly. The chief architect and his assistants were in charge of planning and building. They had to be experts in mathematics, architecture, engineering, and geometry. In addition to the pyramid complex itself, the architects had to provide the living quarters for the workmen, as well as for the priests

The Great Pyramid of Giza

One of the many tasks involved in building the pyramids was making mud-bricks, as is shown in this detail from a New Kingdom wall painting. This painting is from the tomb of the vizier Rekhmira, located in the Valley of the Nobles at Qurna.

who would serve in the Mortuary Temple. The workers also excavated the artificial harbor and the canal that connected it to the Nile. This meant that boats carrying stone blocks could sail right up close to the site, cutting down the distance the blocks needed to be dragged over land.

Keeping Track of Things

Alongside the architects were the officials and their staff of scribes. Their task was to acquire all the different supplies needed to keep the project running and organize its arrival. The officials also had to organize the thousands of workers. A fleet of ships had to be built to transport the great number of workers from all over Egypt to the pyramid site at Giza. Once on site, the thousands of men had to be housed, fed, and kept in good health. A steady supply of food had to

come from the royal storehouses, and an army of cooks, bakers, and brewers had to be assembled. Another vital task for officials was to arrange the transport of the stone blocks by river from their various quarries. Timing was crucial. The Nile flooded every year between mid-June and mid-October. Its waters spread over the land, right up to the desert edge. The aim was to have as many blocks as possible ready

for transport when the waters started rising. In addition to men, food, and stone, supplies of wood, metal, and ropes were also needed for the workmen's tools and equipment.

The Skilled Workforce

Foremost among the craftsmen were the masons.
Unskilled

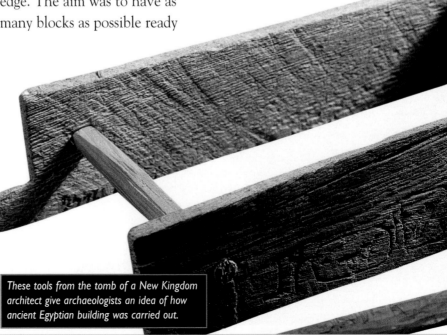

These tools from the tomb of a New Kingdom architect give archaeologists an idea of how ancient Egyptian building was carried out.

Tales & Customs — A Hungry Serpent

The ancient Egyptians believed that when the Sun god Ra sailed through the Underworld at night, he would encounter a monstrous serpent called Apophis, who would try to swallow him. Sometimes the god Set defeated Apophis for Ra. Other times, the Great Cat of Ra would pounce on the snake and chop it into pieces with a knife. However the serpent was defeated each night, as long as Ra survived, he would be be born again the next morning in the east.

men could cut blocks from quarries, but experts had to choose the right stone and show the laborers how to pry blocks from the quarry. In addition, skilled workers were needed to shape and finish each block.

Egypt's best sculptors were also needed. The inside walls of the Causeway were covered with fine relief sculptures and there would have been dozens of statues of Khufu in both the Mortuary and the Valley Temples. All tools, sleds, and ropes constantly needed repairing or replacing, so many carpenters, metalsmiths, and ropemakers were employed on site, too. Archaeologists have found the remains of the workshops where some of the craftsmen worked at Giza.

Boatbuilders, as illustrated in this temple painting from Sakkara, were among the thousands of workers required at Giza. The Nile River was the most effective route for delivering equipment and supplies.

Other Workers

Although they did not work on the actual building site, boat-builders were of vital importance to the pyramid-building project. Large wooden boats were required for carrying the heavy blocks of stone from quarry to the pyramid site.

As native Egyptian trees did not make good-quality timber, lumber had to be imported. The best source for it was the country now called Lebanon, which had forests of magnificent cedar trees. People working on the pyramid sometimes fell ill and, of course, there were accidents resulting in broken bones or crushed limbs. The king took responsibility for workers' welfare and employed doctors to care for them on site.

The Great Pyramid of Giza

Unskilled Workforce

In the days before money was invented, people used the barter system, which was based on the exchange of goods and services. During that time, taxes had to be paid in goods and services. Farmers gave part of their crops and craftsmen gave some of the things they made to the king as taxes. It is also generally assumed that people had to pay the king a tax in the form of work—in a mine or quarry on a royal building project.

Of course, not everyone would have been called up for service at once. Across the country, probably only one out of one hundred people were called up at any given time. So, once you had done a stint, it would be a long time before your services would be required again. Officials traveled around the country with lists of men who were due to do their work tax. These men were shipped to Giza, where they served for three months at a time. While serving, they were fed, housed, clothed, and provided with oil (to keep their skin clean and supple) by the king.

Compulsory Effort

The best time for a man who owned a farm to do his work tax was when the Nile flood had covered his fields, but to get the pyramid completed there needed to be unskilled workers laboring throughout the year. Arrangements would have to be made for others to do their work outside the flood season.

It is estimated that there would usually be about 20,000 unskilled laborers on a pyramid site at one time. Recent excavations at Giza have shown that the men were well fed. Besides bread and beer—the basic items in any ancient Egyptian meal—the workmen also enjoyed a wide variety of meat, fish, vegetables, and fruit. Each "gang" of ten people probably bunked together in the barracks.

This figurine shows a potter at work. Potters would have been among the many craftsmen at Giza.

The Giza Gangs

Each gang had a name. Some names did not inspire respect. For instance, one gang working on the third Giza pyramid, that of King Menkawre, called themselves "The Drunkards of Menkawre." There may have been some rivalry between gangs to see who could shift the most blocks, inspiring some of them to take names like "The Enduring Gang." These men believed that by working to guarantee the journey of their god-king to the Afterlife, they were ensuring their own future in the Next World.

This photograph illustrates the kind of large-scale bread-making that would have had to have taken place at Giza to feed the thousands of pyramid workers.

They had served him, and therefore, he would see that they were well treated after death—as he had cared for them while they worked on his pyramid. At the end of their three-month stints, the men would be shipped home

This wall painting shows the sheer numbers required to transport a colossal statue.

and a new batch would arrive. It was possible, however, that, if a man was a landless laborer at home, he might choose to train and become one of the permanent labor force on the pyramid site.

Tales & Customs — You Silly Goose!

One Egyptian legend that was circulating by the time of the Middle-Kingdom period tells of the great priest-magician Dedi. When Dedi was the grand old age of 110 years old, Khufu summoned him to Court to demonstrate his powers. At the King's command, a goose was brought in and its head was cut off. Dedi recited various prayers and spells which were said to result in the head and body of the goose moving back together and joining together once more. The goose then ran off honking.

The Giza Plateau is one of the most popular destinations for the modern tourist. With its towering pyramids—or the "Mountains of Pharaoh," as early Arab writers called them—Giza attracts two million tourists every year. Daytime attractions include exploring the pyramids, camel rides, and shopping. Evening entertainment includes the "Sound and Light" show and, occasionally, an open-air production of Verdi's opera Aida.

Journey in Comfort

The journey between Egypt's capital, Cairo, and Giza used to be through open fields. Indeed, when the Empress Eugenie of France went to Egypt for the opening of the Suez Canal in 1869, the Khedive Ismail, the ruler of Egypt at the time, had to build a road through farmland, just so she could visit the pyramids comfortably in her carriage.

In the later 20th century, however, Cairo started growing rapidly, and its suburbs now sprawl right up to the foot of the desert cliff on which the pyramids are built. With the hundreds of apartments, hotels, and villas came spectacular traffic jams and long delays during the drive between the center of Cairo and Giza. To solve these problems, a new road system has been built, making the journey quicker and easier.

Follow the Crowd

The day starts early in Giza. By eight o'clock, hoards of tourists are arriving via buses, vans, and

Luxury hotels have been built right up to the foot of the Giza Plateau.

taxis. More and more visitors arrive during the day. When a cruise ship docks in Alexandria, hundreds of passengers are driven on an exhausting but exhilarating day trip that takes in the magnificent sites at Cairo and Giza. The plateau is even more crowded than usual with these extra tourists. Besides the tourists there are usually also several groups of excited Egyptian school children studying the history of their country firsthand.

In order to reduce damage to the inside of the Great Pyramid, the number of tourists allowed in is now limited (see p. 44). Twice a day, only one hundred tickets are sold. It is not advisable for people who have breathing problems, a bad back, or stiff knees to go into the Great Pyramid. In some passages, people must walk while bent over, and the Grand Gallery is a very steep climb.

One of the many groups of tourists that visit the Giza Plateau each day gathers around its guide to hear about the Sphinx and Khafre's Valley Temple.

The Camel Corps—shown here attending an annual festival—are part of the security forces that guard the pyramids at Giza.

Tourists Beware

Once out of their buses, tourists are pounced on by salespeople offering everything from postcards, stamps, sunhats, and guide books to cool drinks, Bedouin headscarves, model pyramids, toy camels, and imitation ancient Egyptian jewelry fig-

Tales & Customs — Khufu's Royal Line

An Egyptian legend states that, when questioned about the future by Khufu, the priest-magician Dedi told the King that only his son and grandson would reign after him. In fact, the main male line of Khufu's family did die out with his grandson. However, the next (Fifth) dynasty of kings were descended from his granddaughter and a great-granddaughter. Dedi's prophecies about the kings of the Fifth Dynasty are written in the "Westcar Papyrus." Ra is said to have aided these kings in their rise to power.

Verdi's opera Aida, which is set in Egypt, is often performed in an open-air theater before the grand backdrop of the pyramids.

urines. Besides the salespeople, there are people with camels, horses, and donkeys for hire.

A New "View Point"

After exploring the Great Pyramid, visitors often drive around the back of the pyramids to a desert ridge that has become known as "View Point." Because of their great size, it is very difficult to photograph all three pyramids together, but at View Point it is possible. If visitors do not go inside the Great Pyramid, they may choose to go inside one of the other major Giza pyramids, Khafre or Menkawre.

A visit to the boat museum, which houses the funeral boat of Khufu, is also an extraordinary sight. As visitors enter the museum, they are required to put canvas slippers over their shoes. This is to protect the wooden floor from being damaged by people's shoes. Staircases and galleries wind all around the boat.

Many tourists have photos taken of themselves taking rides on camels, which are known as the "ships of the desert."

34

Tales & Customs — Lord of the Boat

Coptic legend tells of a king who built the Giza pyramids and filled them with treasure, statues, and scrolls full of scientific knowledge. He did this because he had dreamed that one day there would be a catastrophic flood that would destroy everything. Only those who joined the "Lord of the Boat" would survive. No one knows who the Lord of the Boat was believed to be, but many think he was thought to be a combination of the biblical Noah and the Egyptian god Ra.

On a winter day, when there can be many clouds, some tourists linger into the late afternoon. If they are very lucky, Sun rays sometimes shine through the clouds, outlining one or another of the pyramids with an aura of light. This sight recalls the spell in the *Pyramid Texts* that promises the king a ramp of sunbeams, upon which he can walk to heaven.

Nighttime Entertainment

As the daytime tourists leave, the Giza Plateau prepares itself for a new influx of people. Every evening, there are "Sound and Light" shows at the pyramids. Usually, the two performances given each night are in different languages, in order to cater to tourists from around the world, as well as Cairo residents.

Behind the pyramids there is an open-air theater. Here, perform-ances of Verdi's great romantic opera, *Aida*, which is set in ancient Egypt, are sometimes staged. *Aida* was actually written to celebrate the opening of the Suez Canal. There is no more dramatic backdrop for this opera than the pyramids themselves.

The Sphinx glowing in the unearthly lights of a "Sound and Light" performance at Giza.

A newly discovered inscription shows that Khufu reigned for at least twenty-seven years, not twenty-four as was thought earlier. Even so, his pyramid was not quite finished when he died. The Subterranean Chamber, for example, was not ready, but work stopped. The funeral, which was the whole purpose of the pyramid, had to take place so the eternal cycle of offerings to the King's spirit could begin.

Death by the Nile

No records exist that explain how an Egyptian king's body was prepared for burial. However, we do know about the process for wealthy commoners. The king's would have been essentially the same—just on a grander scale.

When Khufu died, the whole palace would have been plunged into very noisy mourning, with people wailing, tearing their hair, and throwing dirt over their heads. The embalmers would then arrive, accompanied by a priest known as a "lector priest," who would have recited prayers and rituals, and two priestesses known as the "kites." They would then have taken the body,

The mummy of Nefer from the tomb of Nefer and Waty at Sakkara is so well-preserved that his facial features are quite clearly intact even after thousands of years.

perhaps on one of the boats discovered at Giza (see pp. 40–41), downstream to the pyramid site.

Mummification

Khufu's body would then be taken to a tent-building called an "ibu." There, the body purification and prayers would have

taken place and the embalming process begun. The brain and the internal organs would be removed and taken away to be preserved separately. Once these messy stages of the process were completed, the ibu could then be destroyed without leaving a trace. The body would then be moved to the wabet, or "Pure Place," a mud-brick building also near the river. The wabet used for Khufu would not be the same one used for his subjects. His was attached to his Valley Temple, perhaps on the flat roof. There, his body would have been covered with a special salt called natron, which would draw out all the water. His body would then be wrapped up in linen bandages. The whole process took seventy days and

An Arab legend describes the first raid on the Great Pyramid as occurring in A.D. 820. According to the legend, when Caliph al-Mamun's men broke into Khufu's pyramid, they were greeted by a golden cockerel, inlaid with precious stones, that actually flapped its wings and crowed. There was also a body covered in rubies in a gold box and a water jar that never ran dry. However, according to the highly respected Arab historian Abu Szalt, who went into the pyramid with Mamun's men, all they really found were a few bones.

This Old Kingdom relief from Sakkara shows people bearing offerings to the king's tomb.

perfumes and cosmetics, tools and weapons, and jewelry and treasure. At some point—perhaps in the Mortuary Temple, amid clouds of incense—a special ceremony called "Opening of the Mouth" was performed to give the dead king the power to speak, hear, smell, eat, breath, and move. He had become an "effective" spirit.

This New Kingdom painting shows a priest performing the "Opening of the Mouth" ceremony on a mummy.

was accompanied by prayers, rituals, and magic spells.

The Funeral

Finally, the body would have been carried in a wooden coffin to the tomb accompanied by an entourage, along with an army of servants carrying offerings of every conceivable thing that the king would need to enjoy the Next World—food of all kinds, wine, beer, furniture, clothes,

CHAPTER 7

Uncovering the Past

After Christianity became the official religion of the Roman Empire, ancient Egyptian hieroglyphics were no longer used. Ancient knowledge, ideas, and customs were forgotten. Strange stories were told around the Giza pyramids: They were built to escape Noah's flood, or they were the granaries built by Joseph to store grain in the seven years of plenty, or they were a storehouse to protect books of secret wisdom.

Europeans Discover Egypt

Because of the bad relations between Christians and Muslims during the Crusades of the Middle Ages—which were fought between 1095 and 1291—very few Europeans visited Egypt for several centuries. Still, a few Europeans did make it, at least to Giza, between the 16th and 18th centuries. They published accounts of their adventures but, in the days before cameras, the illustrations were rarely accurate. Everything changed after 1798, when Napoleon Bonaparte invaded Egypt. Napoleon was impressed by the Giza pyramids. Just before a crucial battle, it is said that he pointed to the pyramids and shouted, "Soldiers! Forty centuries look down upon you from these pyramids."

Jean-Francois Champollion's ideas about how to read hieroglyphics were published in 1822.

Attached to his army, Napoleon had a group of scholars, whose task was to travel throughout Egypt, producing accurate descriptions and drawings of all its ancient monuments. The publication of their great *Description de l'Egypte*, combined with Champollion's discovery of how to read ancient hieroglyphics, caught people's imagination. This started an interest in ancient Egyptian history that continues to this day.

Ruthless Collectors

In the 19th century, people went to Egypt to explore the monuments and to bring back artifacts, whether for museums or their own private collections. People were fascinated by beautiful, magnificent (and valuable) works of art, such as statues, reliefs, paintings, and jewelry. Some people even

In the 19th century, scholars swarmed over Egypt, exploring its great monuments, including Abu Simbel (pictured).

on a measurement he called the "pyramid inch." Smyth believed that the measurements of the pyramid, its chambers, and its passages, were the result of a set of prophecies, inspired by God, that foretold events in the history of the world, confirmed certain events in the Bible, and revealed such scientific details as the circumference of Earth. Smyth and his followers have been dubbed "pyramidiots" by scholars.

thought it was impressive to own an ancient mummy. A great deal of damage and robbery resulted. One man even blasted his way into Khafre's pyramid with dynamite.

Incredible Theories

People have always been fascinated by the pyramids, especially Khufu's Great Pyramid, and the rest of the Giza group. Nineteenth century archaeologists analyzed the Great Pyramid—measuring, drawing, and recording. But there were those who found it difficult to believe that the Great Pyramid was "just" a tomb. One such enthusiast was Charles Piazzi Smyth. Having measured every bit of the pyramid, he decided that the whole thing was based

In the 19th century, many theories arose about the mystical origins of the Great Pyramid. In this illustration, Egyptian priests survey the stars from a chamber within the Great Pyramid.

Tales & Customs — In His Father's Image

Hordedef was one of Khufu's sons. Hordedef was himself revered as a wise man, but only a fragment of his teachings have survived. In them, he gives his readers practical advice on how to behave and recommends that they prepare for the future, both in this world and the next. Legend says he discovered some secret books of wisdom. These books are said to have been incorporated into the Book of the Dead, an important text that was used in burials during the New Kingdom.

Tales & Customs — A Talking Sphinx?

The Sphinx fascinated the early European explorers. Johannes Helferich, a Geramn who was in Egypt in the later 16th century, claimed that there was a secret passage in the Sphinx, in which priests would hide and fool the people into believing the Sphinx was speaking to them. The fact that, in his book, Helferich illustrated the Sphinx as female (representing the goddess Isis) did not do much for his credibility. And, to this day, no passages or chambers have been found in the Sphinx.

All the King's Boats

By the mid 20th century, five boat-shaped graves around the Great Pyramid had been known for hundreds of years. Then, in 1954, two more pits were discovered. Both were roofed by huge limestone slabs. When the roof was removed from the first pit, the dismantled remains of a large wooden boat were revealed. As archaeologists removed the boat, piece by piece, they realized that, thanks to Egypt's dry climate, the wood was in such miraculously good condition that it might be possible to rebuild the 4,500-year-old boat. The boat was made of cedar wood and the planks were originally lashed together with ropes. There were 1,224 separate parts to reassemble, and the project took many years.

The earliest Nile boats were made of bundles of papyrus reeds. Though made of cedar wood, the prow and stern of Khufu's boat are carved to represent the bound bundles of reeds used in earlier times.

Only a few pieces were too warped or decayed to use. Those pieces were replaced by modern replicas. Modern rope had to be used, although the archaeologists did find a large coil of the original rope. The boat now rests in its own museum, which also covers the pit where it was found. The boat is 140 feet (43 m) long, a vessel of elegance and breathtaking beauty.

In 1985, a tiny camera was lowered through a hole drilled in one of the roof blocks of the second pit. This pit also contains a dismantled boat, which has been left in its pit. By Khufu's time, burying boats was not actually a new idea. The remains of boats, or the pits that once contained them, have been found in royal graves dating back to Dynasty I. It was certainly unusual, however, for Khufu to have had seven.

Sailing into Eternity

It seems likely that Khufu's seven boats were intended for

A Middle-Kingdom model of a Nile boat. Note the square sail and large steering oar.

different purposes. The boat that has been reconstructed may have been the actual vessel that carried Khufu's dead body to his pyramid. If so, that would have made it a very holy object that could not be used again. Perhaps by taking it apart and burying it, the ancient Egyptians thought its power would be safely contained.

The other boats may have been used by the royal family in life, and they may have been buried so the family could go on using them in the Next World.

Sailing with Ra

The Egyptians imagined that, on his journey across the sky, Ra

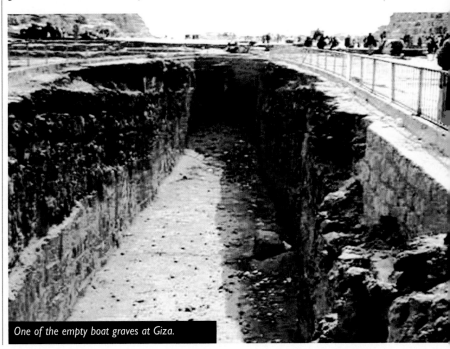

One of the empty boat graves at Giza.

The Great Pyramid of Giza

traveled by boat along a heavenly Nile. When he was reborn in the east each day, he boarded one boat to use on his journey to the west. In the evening, he boarded another boat, which was to take him through the Underworld, bringing light to the realm governed by Osiris, god of the dead, and his subjects. Perhaps the Egyptians thought the king would need boats of his own if he was to travel with Ra across the heavens of the realms of the living and the dead. Clearly, Khufu was not a king who did things incompletely—especially where his own glory and comfort in the Next World were concerned.

Archaeology and Science

In the late 19th century, an archaeologist named Flinders Petrie introduced scientific methods into Egyptian archaeology. Museums and universities mounted expeditions to study sites in depth. George Reisner, Hermann Junker, and Selim Hassan excavated many nobles' tombs at Giza and published their findings in great detail.

During this time, another important development occurred in the study of Egypt's architectural treasures. New rules were introduced about digging in Egypt and the removal of artifacts. Any excavator had to get a license to dig from the Egyptian Antiquities Service, and it was recognized that the objects they found belonged to the Egyptian people. Excavators received a share of their finds, but the best pieces, the unique objects, were kept in Egypt. These rules are still in force.

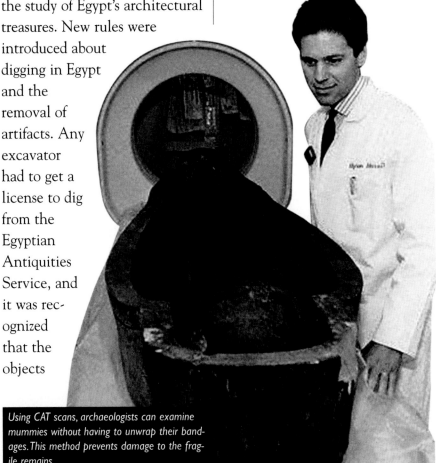

Using CAT scans, archaeologists can examine mummies without having to unwrap their bandages. This method prevents damage to the fragile remains.

Tales & Customs — Secret Names

Each Egyptian god and goddess had a secret name, which was said to be the source of his or her magic powers. One day Ra was stung by a magic scorpion that had been put in his path by his cunning great-granddaughter, Isis. Ra was in agony. Only Isis could cure him. She said she would do so, but only if he told her his secret name. In the end, Ra had to give in, and she cured him. This meant that Isis now possessed Ra's powers as well as her own and, therefore, became the greatest of all magicians.

New Finds at Giza

Archaeology has come a long way since 1880, when Petrie first went to Egypt to measure the Giza pyramids. Today, besides looking for precious artifacts, archaeologists are also looking for things that, although worthless in themselves, are incredibly valuable because of what they can tell us about the lives of ordinary Egyptians, such as the men who built the Great Pyramid.

In the 1980s, new excavations began at Giza and are still going on today. The center of interest is now not the pyramids or the nobles' tombs, but the people who built them. To learn about them, the archaeologists had to look outside the main, sacred areas. They uncovered the workshops, barracks, and kitchens of the thousands who labored to build the magnificent monuments. The work is conducted with great care, so that even tiny things are recovered. Fruit seeds and fish bone, for example, give valuable information about the workmen's diet.

This papyrus from the Book of the Dead shows a deceased person purifying offerings by pouring water over them.

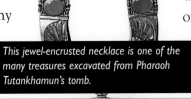

This jewel-encrusted necklace is one of the many treasures excavated from Pharaoh Tutankhamun's tomb.

In Khufu's Shadow

Archaeologists also recovered the cemetery of the men (usually members of the permanent workforce) and their families, who died during the course of construction.

More than one thousand graves have been discovered so far. Interestingly, some of them have small mud-brick pyramids built over the top. These remains, which only a few years ago would have received little attention, are now carefully examined. They reveal details about the person's diet, medical history, and age at death. The worn backbone of one of these men shows that he had once done hard physical labor, presumably hauling stones for the pyramid. But the inscriptions in his tomb reveal that, when he died, he was an important overseer. Some scholars view this find as critical evidence that an ordinary Egyptian could rise up through the ranks of society.

All over the world, people are fascinated by ancient Egypt. Its architecture, furniture, and jewelry have been imitated and adapted for modern tastes. Ancient Egypt has also inspired many films—from great Hollywood biblical epics to horror and sci-fi movies.

Our Duty to the Pharaohs

Once only the very wealthy could afford to visit Egypt. That changed in 1869, when Thomas Cook began offering package holidays in Egypt at modest prices. Now thousands of tourists flock to Egypt every year, and one of the first things they see is the Great Pyramid and the other monuments of the Giza Plateau.

But tourists can damage the very wonders they have come to admire. Roads have been built across sites and buses rumble around, causing vibrations that can damage the monuments. Thousands of feet trampling on ancient pavements put great wear on them, and, at Giza, the pollution from the ever-growing city of Cairo is also a problem. Just as bad is the effect of humans inside a monument. Their breath and perspiration leaves the air damp, which damages the stones.

Efforts are being made to preserve the monuments throughout Egypt, but those lucky enough to visit the ancient sites must also work to preserve them by obeying some simple rules. Don't lean on the walls because the salty sweat from the human body will destroy paint and delicate carvings; don't use flash lights because their beams destroy colors in the paint; and don't carve your name into the walls.

Modern Technology

Increasing numbers of scientific techniques are now available to archaeologists. These help provide a better understanding of the things discovered—right down to the last fish bone, insect-wing case, and seed. Computers are used to analyze information about a ruined building supplied by

A modern craftsman uses ancient techniques to carve a block to repair an ancient building. The building may even have been worked on by his distant ancestors.

Tales & Customs — An End to Famine

During the reign of King Zoser, Egypt suffered seven years of famine. Zoser consulted his wise minister, Imhotep, who told him that the god Khnum was responsible for withholding the Nile's annual flood. Zoser prayed to Khnum, who appeared to him in a dream. The two are said to have made a deal. Zoser agreed to build Khnum a temple and endow it with land and, in return, Khnum promsied to send good floods and bumper harvests. According to legend, this deal ended the seven years of famine.

By leaving the Sphinx uncovered, it has been left vulnerable to the abrasive effects of wind-blown sand. Major repair work has recently been done to preserve it.

the skills of ancient craftsmen and builders, some archaeologists try to make things the way the ancients did. At Giza, they even built a small pyramid to see if their theories about pyramid-building techniques worked in practice. Modern architects sometimes design structures that use pyramid shapes made of modern materials such as concrete, steel, and glass. They are often very impressive, of course, but nothing can compare with the real thing. Gazing up at the mountainous Great Pyramid is a thrilling experience. It truly is one of the wonders of the world.

archaeologists and show us how the building looked when new. Some medical techniques and equipment are also invaluable tools for studying and preserving the past. For example, a CAT scan can be used to show a picture of the body and skeleton of a mummy without the need to remove the bandages and destroy the mummy. Researchers even use tiny cameras that allow them to look inside a body without cutting it open. Soon, advances in recovering ancient DNA will help scientists build up information on the family ties and racial origins of groups of mummies.

Experimental Archaeology

To understand and appreciate

The glass pyramid that was built in front of the Louvre Museum, located in Paris, France.

45

Glossary

afterlife: life after death. Also known by the Egyptians as the "Next World."

Amun: Amun began his rise to power as patron of the kings of Dynasty XII. Later, he was identified with Ra and became Amun-Ra, King of the Gods. The ram was one of his sacred animals.

anthropoid: human-shaped.

Anubis: God of embalming, guardian of the dead. His sacred animal was the jackal.

capstone: the pointed stone placed at the top of a pyramid.

casing blocks: finely cut and polished blocks that make up the outer layer of a pyramid.

cataract: a place where outcroppings of rock interrupt the flow of the Nile. There are six cataracts, the first is at Aswan, and the sixth is just north of Khartoum.

Causeway: in Egyptian pyramid complexes, a roofed passage built of stone that connects the Valley and Mortuary Temples of straight-sided pyramids.

citadel: a fortress built on high ground above a city.

Coptic: related to the branch of the Christian Church that evolved in Egypt; derived from the Greek name for Egypt.

dynasty: a family of rulers.

Hathor: one of Egypt's oldest and most powerful goddesses, a mother who protects her worshippers in this world and the Next World. Her sacred animal was a cow.

Horus: one of Egypt's most ancient gods, Horus was god of the sky and of kingship. The falcon was his sacred bird.

ibu: a tent in which a body was taken in preparation for burial; also called "the place of purification."

Inundation: the Nile River's annual flood. In Egypt, a land with very little rain, people depended on the Nile's annual flood. To stress its importance, it is commonly referred to as "the Inundation."

Isis: an Egyptian goddess who was great-granddaughter of Ra, wife of her brother, Osiris, and mother of Horus. When her husband was murdered, Isis helped restore him to life.

ka: in the ancient Egyptian view, the part of the soul that represents a person's individual personality. It was in human form and needed food and provisions to enjoy the Next World.

Khafre: an ancient Egyptian king, son of Khufu, who built the second pyramid of Giza; known in Greek as Chephren.

Khnum: the god of the First Cataract, controller of the Nile, who fashioned people's bodies and spirits on his potter's wheel.

Khufu: the ancient Egyptian king who built the Great Pyramid of Giza; known in Greek as Cheops.

mastaba: a rectangular tomb, built of stone or mud brick, on the surface of the desert. The body was usually buried in an underground chamber.

Menkawre: an ancient Egyptian king, son of Khafre, who built a pyramid at Giza; known in Greek as Mycerinus.

Mortuary Temple: a temple built against the side of a pyramid in which priests were supposed to make daily offerings to a dead king's spirit for eternity.

mummification: the Egyptian method of preserving the body after death by removing the internal organs, embalming it, and wrapping it in bandages.

Next World: see *afterlife*.

Nubia: the land to the south of Egypt that was an important trading partner for Egypt.

Opening of the Mouth: a ritual performed during an ancient Egyptian funeral that was thought to give the dead person the power to speak, breath, feel, and move.

oracle: a person, usually a priest, through whom a god or goddess is believed to speak and give advice.

Osiris: the Egyptian God of the Dead, ruler of the Underworld who was murdered by his jealous brother, Set, but brought back to life by Isis and Horus, his sister-wife and son. Because he had been resurrected, the ancient Egyptians believed that, through

him, they too would be born again and live for ever.

overseer: the title used by every senior- or middle-ranking official in ancient Egyptian government.

pharaoh: a respectful way of referring to the Egyptian king that became a title during the New Kingdom.

Ra: the Egyptian sun god, whose main temple was at Heliopolis, a few miles north of Memphis. His sacred animal was a bull. Sometimes called "Re."

sarcophagus: a stone coffin.

scribe: an official in ancient Egypt who copied documents and recorded important events in writing.

Sphinx: a representation of the Egyptian Sun god in the form of a creature having a human head and the body of a lion.

stela: an upright slab of stone (or sometimes wood) bearing religious inscriptions or inscriptions that record a special event.

Thoth: the Egyptian god of wisdom and medicine, whose sacred creatures were the ibis and the

baboon, and whose main temple was at Hermopolis.

The Two Lands: the two separate kingdoms—Upper (southern) and Lower (northern) Egypt—that came to form one kingdom. Upper Egypt stretched from the First Cataract to the place where the Nile divides (at which modern Cairo now stands). There, the Nile divides into several channels and flows through Lower Egypt to the Mediterranean Sea.

underworld: in Egyptian mythology, a realm inhabited by the dead, similar to the Christian concept of Hell in that it was believed to be filled with fiery lakes and volcanoes. Every night Ra was believed to sail through this realm and defeat the angry Sun in order to ensure that the Sun rose again on the new day.

Valley Temple: a temple in a pyramid complex located at the point at which the valley meets the desert.

vizier: a major official in ancient Egypt who was in charge of the government and running the pyramid-building project.

Index